Silke, Denis, Georgia, Kasper,
thanks for your help and talent.

For your inspiration,
Sarah, Mike and the Bar Tenders
at Tomsky.

...with Ruby

Beat The Grass

by
Robert Grant

Bibliographische Information der
Deutschen Nationalbibliothek:
Die Deutsche Nationalbibliothek
verzeichnet diese Publikation in der
Deutschen Nationalbibliographie;
detaillierte bibliographische Daten sind
im Internet über http://www.dnb.de
abrufbar.

Herstellung und Verlag:
BoD- Books on Demand, Norderstedt

ISBN 978-3-7481-5874-5

Contents

"I've been totally convinced for twenty, odd years, that I'm just suffering from a comprehensively nervous, breakdown.

Standing within my own morality,
questioning if I really have the time"

(In conversation with Kasper...Berlin, 2018)

Wipe, Fresh

You can tell so much about a writer
by what they clean off their computer
screen and what with.

I just cleaned red wine, tobacco and
other nefarious stains off mine. Using
spit on an old used sock.

It has...and always will be the words
that matter. Not what you're writing on
or with, that validates relevance.

Bums like me

Sometimes I think on my life
as fairly pointless. A day consisting of
walking around the park, sitting in
coffee shops, watching people contend
with more needed aspects of life.

A Police officer on her morning break,
rifling a bagel down neck, whilst
agreeing through a shoulder mounted
radio..slurp, chew, tear.

The suntanned construction worker,
hiding his 11am ice cold beer, smashing
something with something else.

A pressured doctor, screaming at his
telephone, pops pills as breath mints.

Trash men sweating in mid morning sun.

Mother tending annoying child.

Future leaders on school trips, arguing
over plastic toys and salty sticks.

Homeless men selling CD's and tapes
of the Rock Band he used to be, from
a threadbare tartan shopping cart.

Fat shop assistants blowing smoke
through sunlight, whilst expertly
bitching out co-workers and fashion
trends and anything...for all time.

Then me, this observant misanthrope,
nosing my way in, for the splittest
of seconds. Making up words,
on a relentless journey,
towards lies and dirty feet.

So every time I see my life pointless.
I retreat to a bustled train station
report on a world you just don't see.
Rushing through busily ignoring,
the difference in me.

Five minute lives happening
at this solitary someplace.
As I drink a frozen latte,
watching multiple stories...

...Clung to this shinny dampened
pebble, hurtling through infinity,
misunderstanding control for empathy.

Convinced nowhere is coming,
and nowhere is good.

So dance more confidently,

for you're right

not misunderstood.

New Excuse

Head turned,
sucker punched into
thinking I had control.
Amounting to an identical
experience, dismantling promise.

Same excuses
executed by a boastful amateur.
One more chance,
to throw it all away.

Same embarrassments
to float the informer
raising his chin,
awaiting the blow down, this
once rested contender waits.

Left only to recant
arrogant statements
amid computerised apologies,
to people he doesn't actually know.

Waiting for morning

...of these clean mornings
before the chaos starts.
This town air rests neatly
on rendered skies.
Last night's mistakes hidden
under a facade of
white washed trees
awaiting exhaust fumes.

Hung over patrons,
uninterested in the hustle.
Actors waiting to transform, hastily
coughing out last night cigarettes,
dressing up to become
someone less important
and never understanding
that statement.

Road workers sharpening their tools,
trash men collect.

Money drones sharpening their minds
for blunting.
Nurses and bus boys
stand in bussed lines,
as bar tenders come off
last night's exhausting shift.

All things happening
as a poet sits in his
comfortably fumed office.
Gazing through unwashed windows,
on undeveloped land
upon which
idiots can shop
and chat and dream.

All of them expecting
that great thing to happen.
The spectacular now,
waiting to be bought,
wrangled from the closed hand
of a baby
ingesting culture through gurgles.

They wait to be brought into existence
by people like me.
The actor wanting to be made iconic,
nurses waiting to be made heroes,
bartenders waiting for the next big tip.

As the world is waiting to wake up, I
sit amongst the chaos,
amidst all these stories,
with nothing to do, but wait
and hope to see
something different.

Crane

Every time I see someone
working on the street, shovelling trash,
cutting concrete weeds,
a small part of me feels jealous.

Wants to be them.

Wants to come home at the end of a
long hard day, exhausted, stinking to
high heaven,
falling into a hot bath, then bed.

Tired from puckered snobbish sneers.

The honesty of the whole thing
invites me. The truculent nature of
hammer to ground appeals,
until this day rolled round.

Now warmly sat.

I see a seventy year old crane operator
struggling in the rain,
pain protruding with every dip.
I'm happy to be sat here surveying.

Watching on with first class ambiguity.

Bloody Ball

She's here
It...came.
Into this world,
a place I also find myself.
Scared at first,
didn't know how
this bloodied ball would act, or
make me act.
Blind to what it was to laugh, but
she would teach me.
Show me the obvious simplicity
of everything I'd forgotten
about being a child.
How a simple laugh
was more powerful than a
forced one.
She confirmed the thing
I fear the most...

      ...that there is beauty
here...

...in this most ruined of places,
in this most distant of hearts,
I too, am beautiful.
This (now made) super hero
is splendid,
for as long as she shows me
those wonders,
I will be the best father she has.

Knowing I created her laughs,
her joyful expressions,
educes hairs to dance on
my forearm.
Makes me recognise
I still have fight, every time
I tickle her belly
with my beard.

She'll read this
sometime in the future.
Laugh with friends about Papa's itchy
beard, his simple dress sense
and courts of distraction.

Recant stories of times
in the past
when everything made sense.
Just as it does for me
as I talk to you know.
In this realm,
I've spent my life living.

We laughed a lot,
cried and loved a lot.
You shouted and stomped
your tiny foot.
Stuck lip gloss up your vagina,
then denied all knowledge
"it was a monster" you said
and continued stroking
that stuffed horses mane.

I want you to read this,
when older, and know,
that you saved my life,
just as much as I
constantly save yours now.
That, when you were born

we were equally scared
and covered in bloody questions
answered with first wink
of cherished pink eye.

The first time you lied.
The second time you won
by manipulating Mummy,
I conceded and knew
my baby was born.

My only wish being,
a more lofty expression
as these first tasks, are eternally yours.
My promise being
to try not to fuck it up
too much...
                    ...as you smile
and rumble your tiny
chin at me.

Hat

I spent two and a half minutes,
standing in front of a silver framed
full length mirror.

Arranging and rearranging
a small cotton hat. For some reason
unknown at the time.

Trying front, back and front.
Placing different angles, creating
nothing new.

Realising that I have a lot of
free time on my hands and that
you can write poetry about anything.

Eyes Closed

One by one they fall.
Way sided as if
made of paper.
Floating on the surface
for a while,
only to dissipate
and disperse
when a flush
is applied.

These idiots,
making statements,
they don't understand.
Saying nonsense words
in order of laughs
but it's easy to laugh
at fools as they
try and avoid drowning.

Stretching heads back,
into a sun that

doesn't want them.
Giving useless information,
to an audience
that doesn't want to hear it.

Making points that have
already been made better.
We wish their mouths would close
as well their eyes.
Dreams rested on
ever understanding
anything original.

A Better Idea

Another week is done,
another pittance made,
coffee drunk,
friends made
and lost
yet, I still sit here
the same man,
same problems.
For that
and only that
has not changed.
I am;
a little older,
fatter,
more unwise
tired
and contorted
by the bias I feel
towards idiots
masquerading as
the intelligentsia.

These,
one day heroes,
whose moment
will never come, yet
they feel that this
borrowed time,
is truly on their side.
As I sit,
quietly...in this place.
I wonder if they know
how unimportant
they are to me.
How insignificant
in my big scheme
they are...as I
am truly in theirs.
We sit on this
merry-go-round,
circulating
the lack
of a better idea.
Only hoping not to
bump into
one another again.

First of few

My brain feels lazy,
words seam fattened and
as unnecessary as that
lethargic dance music
playing the background,
on this first day back
to writing...to thinking,
everything fat and flatulent.

This cool, well lit place
slithering music to my subconscious.
Too purposeful to be ignored,
too hummed to concentrate.
Melancholically massaging my
imagination to sleep.
Knowing this book is
too thick to write in and
acknowledging the excuse.

These ink blot hands,
scribes notes of self loathing,

even if I'm doing what I know
I really should.
Clawed words to a page, in light
too thin to grasp fully,
pages sit fat and painfully
under-rehearsed.

My brain is lazy,
words fattened, thoughts unused
in a mind of excuses
now nostalgically flatulent.
Electronic sounds
pumping stomach
with gusto, then to gas.
Letting out a methane warning cry
as just for a second
the coffee shop sits still.

Restoring my sense of humour,
a smile creeps back in.
Followed by retort and
conclusion of important
sounding words.
It has started again,

on this first day back to writing.
With clawed hands,
BEATing tight hairy chest.

Shaking

So shaky,
	feel unsteady on legs,
			but why is unclear.

	I'm minding my own business,

wonder why I feel so uncomfortable

in the place.

			Suddenly noticing

that one stool leg is

	shorter than the other three.

Bubbles

The day before I fell apart,
I found myself at a poetry show.

First, a black poet stands proud on
stage, then spends twenty minutes
telling me he's black.

Then comes a homosexual poet...also
telling me nothing I didn't already know.
Recalls a story about waking up with
a condom hanging out of his ass.

Then up comes a feminist poet, making
me feel bad for something or other,
then comes a Christian...come Hipster.

I stand in the audience,
bemused by the spectacle.
Realising how little I've learnt and
how little they've made me think.

Exuding confident from bravado of
the misjudged or underappreciated.
They are right, we are wrong...that's
how it is and/or ever will be.

I can see they think they're doing
something noble or valid.
Not realising that the only way to get
anything from their work, is to be black,
gay, female and/or Christian.

I can only imagine the uproar
if my white heterosexual persona,
read a poem about leaving
a condom in some random girl's ass.

If I said all women were pigs
and terribly oppressive monsters.
If I said that through volume alone
there can't be one true god.

The commotion if I made the point
that with their misguided words
they are keeping, the operant alive.

Keeping the destructive past
awake, when really it's time to sleep
and move on.

My name is called last and I head up to
stage, microphone before me like shot
gun in my mouth.

Totally forgetting my set...I stand
looking at the hipsters,
the dead heads waiting
for a just cause to be presented.

These followers of trends and tattoo
styles, just wanting to tell me I'm wrong.
As I start telling, same old middle aged,
white, heterosexual tales.

Now tinged with the sorrow of
presenting the cliché,
I leave stage,
return to my table
and stand counting bubbles
in my now warm beer.

Haikus

1.

Arrogance has gone,
stripped back to time before,
I first knew myself.

2.

Drinking is not mine,
I will lose my life to it
I have no control.

3.

Finding beauty is
sometimes difficult enough.
Greed is simply there.

4.

I have been writing
for twenty two minutes now.
What have I to show?

5.

Is this a Haiku?
Or have I truly got the
syllable count wrong?

6.

Doubt is a warm hand
providing truth that you still
care about your art.

7.
Dragons do exist.
I am one post consumption
to curious cats.

8.
Running my hands through
what brain I have left, I'm stunned
by a lack of truth.

Just Masturbating Monkeys

What will this world have me do,
when it's ripped off my skin
left me standing naked in the night,
watching monochrome moments
in free fall, as I spin towards infinity
rejecting the man I see on reflection.

When all I have to show
for a life spent dreaming are;
liver spot on back of hand
black spots rampantly surfacing
when conflicted thoughts
come to running once more,
a motley parade of mimicry
behind blanket walls of tear.

When we've locked all hopes of solution
in that black plasma box
adorning my bed room,

adorning my heart,
swallowing down the key,
whilst most bent in knee
as they take away my vanity
pumping hard from behind.

When all it really comes down to are
cheapened version of sanity,
credit card solutions for
greeting card holidays,
nothing more or less than a
21st century one world state
punching feed bars for pellets
in suburban shopping malls.

When sometimes I think they've got it
right those terrorists freedom birds
standing to put up a fight,
giving us back the same hardship
we gave them first,
screaming 'God will save us all' as we
burst forth our superior fighting force
and blow the skins of children
playing football in the park.

When opinion is no longer counted,
no one stands up, no one starts
shouting we all just sit silent,
gag mouthed in solitude because
we don't want to rock the boat
shake the tree, say anything to allude
to our true feelings.

When all I can do is
write a few words down
for preacher corner audiences
on a Monday, just before noon,
when all the people that
should be listening are
locked in cattle cars
whoring out their lives, so
fat men may grows fatter.

When every day is a
question of motivation, of
relevant ambition, so closed to
where we really should be
we walk, face to the floor,
listening intently to successes

rehashing other peoples
fantastic experiences.

When the alternative generation
hides in bog standard impressions,
those individual expressions
coming from H&M with a receipt
a name on my feet,
brand stamped across my heart.

When all I can hope is
that a word or two seep in,
a rhyme hits land on a shore,
so far from where we really should be
that the concept of normality is lost.
What will the world have me do,
but stand, naked in *this* night,
raped of imagination
with energy only
to ask
why.

(First Published in 2008 as 'Naked' Still relevant)

Left...waiting

Interrupted by normality.
Caffeine kick,
mouth dry,
pop technology.

Girls on balconies,
having excited conversations.
Kids with teachers,
squeaking shanties in French.

Thinned blood,
circulates muddled mind.
Hands cold, head hot,
liver cramp.

Remembering lies told,
time wasted, whilst wasted.
Frivolous friendships fade,
memories reset.

I, the champion of nothing,
their contender from nowhere.
Knows really he's
frittered his time once again.

That Woman

Stop it, you fool,
playing with your hair,
repositioning your top.

Stop acting out
pre-rehearsed spiel
that you are important and beloved.

Just let me enjoy my coffee,
this morning,
this seat.

Sit peacefully
for just a minute,
so I may catch my breath.

Stop looking around
for everyone
to lovingly notice.

Stop expressing frustration
through arm waves, and
branded wealth metaphors.

Stop looking up
from your phone
with complete surprise every time.

Stop pouting at pictures.
As, no one else knows
the joke.

Stop being the mother atop
the climbing frame wanting
adoration for being the best one.

Just be normal, you fool.
Be there, at your table
drinking coffee and relaxing.

Stop longingly looking around
for the approval
that really won't come.

Stop acting under oversized sunglasses,
starring straight back at me...as if
disgusted by my attention.

I know I fuel your reflection,
in lieu of anything
more interesting.

Retro

I feel retro sat amongst these laptops,
with book and fountain pen.
Maybe retro is the wrong word,
technophobic a more accurate
description.

Open eyes down. Plug in, drop out,
converted to the new powered
generation. Writing, emailing, insta-
something, buying comics,
not to read.

I stop, for a second and wonder if
their house is being watched, hence
coming here. This place is where you sit,
enjoy coffee, sometimes
with cookies.

This all coming from a man scribbling in
an old tatty book. Who looks just as
stupid as they do.

Only thing going for him,
is that at least he's retro!

Spots

I live behind your love,
in holes like liver spots.

Hoping it's not the end of
the only reason I've got.

Wild

Stay wild...be crazy.
No matter what, keep that wink inside.
Jolt awake, sleep badly.
Live up to every cliché possible.

For when your time is gone
and you're left with a bladder that
doesn't work, without legs to hold you.
Let those wild little memories return.

It happens to everyone,
the great trick of life. Envisioning
your future to a 2.0 version of
no person that ever existed.

Don't regret the thousands of lies you
have told, to a hundred strangers in
bars. On those nights when you
ventured out, to tell lies and get drunk.

For those thousand lies brought you
ever closer to being honest with
yourself, nights blurring together,
harassing the day.

Extend a middle finger nightly.
Confirm that you won't, quietly filter
into piss bags and standardised
beige serving trays.

Kick your legs up and tell some lies.
Run naked down train platforms,
screaming "I am here" and ensure
everyone hears you.

Knowing fully that you are existing.
Then stop being dumb and get back
down to work. For crazy exists in the
courtyard of every standard facade.

When your ticket is inevitably punched,
price paid for this life you've lived.
You'll have but time for one wild wink,
before eyes creak to closed.

So stay crazy, you beautiful little beasty.
For you're right to live it loud.

Unabashed, irreverent

come screaming in the night.

Water Cooler

Drowning in symptoms,
the old sad man still needs
to get high in order
to hear his demon.

That guy is a fallacy,
a character
invented by necessity,
underwhelmed by normality.

Pathetically thinking
he still has a voice.
Yet amazed that he
has come so far.

Never going back
to office politics or
pre-packaged
tuna fish sandwiches.

Metaphors about Sex

After my second book , (Naked in the coffee house) came out, I sent copies home for friends and family.

Comes my Monday morning phone call from Mum.

"Hello dear...how was your weekend?" maternal warmth exuded.

"Hi Mum how's it going with you?"

"I'm good" she answers "Got your book today"

"Great and what do you think?"

"Yes...just one question...Why does it always have to be about sex?"

"No Mum, it's not that I'm actually sitting Naked in a Coffee House...it's a metaphor"

"A what?"

I then spend the next twenty minutes explaining what a metaphor is and how the title of the book is just that, mirroring the state of the world that I see before me. As I sit, stripped and slapped.

How I question this dumb down mentality...reducing everyone to conflicted ideology, impressed upon them by internet trends.
How I felt differently...how the world is an allegory for the un-spontaneous and benefits un-originality, that sometimes I want to shake sense into every Ipad using Über-feminist for being so damn sexist and that the world bares no semblance to any reality that I want to

be involved in. Our hand cart has
already been burnt and will remain
torched as long as we don't call for
some sense of normality, as the deluded
dance in the embers until their feet,
becoming ash blackened and deformed.

"You understand what I mean?" I ask,
dry mouthed but confident.

"OH yeah...I get that" she answers
through a yawn "But why does it always
have to be about sex?"

"How's the weather Mum?" I ask, taking
a seat.

Having two sips of coffee,
with a wide loving smile on my face.

Ruby's question

"Where was I before I was here?"
asked Ruby, scouring the car floor
for a cuddly pink tiger
called Jerry.

My lack of answer was not to be
childishly cruel, but because
I didn't want my ignorance
to lie to her.

Piss

After twenty minute
of walking around my flat
talking to myself,
I finally realise that
I'm the crazy guy
I used to know as a child.

The guy who lived up the road
from my mother's house,
who always seemed to be
answering leading questions
on a chat show with
no audience or host.

Time passing him by.
 As he twitches through,
more blurred days
than anyone who has ever lived.
With piss stained grey trousers
and threadbare socks.

Not giving one small fuck,
for he's done more than
most will ever know or want to know
with varying types of scum,
that only show business can drag up
from its lungs, on mornings after.

His weakening bladder making him
scratch his balls, as dried piss makes him
smell like a drunk bum, asleep
on a tatty park bench
with flies circulated
an unclean rectum.

The words that do erupt his mouth,
such utter nonsense,
for he doesn't realise no one heard
the question from that
orange chat show host.
Who's lines are being fed
from behind closed screens
through an ear piece.

I have become that guy. Crazy and un-
muted. Unable to keep myself
clean, as I shuffle around my flat,
in full view of no one, washing piss
off my hands, talking to my imagination.
Comprehending the comfort
and acting accordingly.

Smoked Hook

This hook in my hand
that I just can't shake.
Sitting before me gleefully
smiling it's toothless parade.

Its boring conversation
with the same people,
same events repeated
to distraction.

From what though
I'm truly unsure
and for what reason
only the hook knows.

Else

The greatest challenge in life
is to realise who you truly are.

Most spend their lives
trying to be someone else,
a foolish perception of how
they imagine themselves.

Reality is always more simple,
if uneasy to except.

Sugar Line

I dropped my kid off at school
this morning, with a cake
baked the night previous.
She peeled back the tin foil covering
to reveal a rectangle with
a three in the middle,
constructed of colourful
sugar covered candy.

The plumped noises in her class,
jumped, joyfully
as my heart sank.
In unison these three years olds
wrangled the sweets from on top,
jiggering their collective excitement
to the corporate beat
already imprinted.

Whilst manufacturers of insulin shots
rubbed their hands
with keen parents silence,

a welcome break
from the constant noise
generated when sugar is added
to the mix. Erupting from orifices
front and back.

Drug imprinting coming from those
helpless parents at a very early age,
only difference being
the price of the drug goes up.
Become more powerful and destructive,
as sugar won't cut it forever,
sped hearts skipping beats as organised
gangsters obtain sleek expensive cars.

These bouncing children,
now resembling an EKG output,
the sugar line running
from mouth to stomach
to arm to heart.
Stopped in its tracks by
this innocent mornings
adolescent mistake.

One Time
(for the cheap seats)

Don't miss me
when I'm gone.
Know that you
were everything to me.
No matter who you are
or how well
we knew one another.
If you're my wife,
ex-lover, friend,
baby Ruby,
or someone reading this.
Know that I had everything.
More than most but no one
had more. I had the best
friends and fans and family.
For it's the only one you get.

You can change friends,
god only knows
I've done that over my time.

You can change jobs and
circumstances like shoes
on a hot day, like
bath water on a cold.
I had every experience
I wanted, every
hand shake meant something,
every tear tasted different.

Now that I'm gone
I take the widest
of smiles with...knowing
that these words
still exist.
Know that
my life belonged to you,
you meant more to me
than even I could say.
Now that all
is said and definitely
done, this poem
will go on.
People will still see my work,
will remember

that time once
and my Baby Ruby
had me as a Dad.
For better, most times,
I did what I could.

For now just remember
that time we laughed
so hard beer came out
of our noses. That time
you read that thing
I wrote, which made you
cry. Or that time
we kissed in the dirty
toilet stall in that
hot nightclub under
the bridge. My life
was full of oddities,
tangled conversational flatulence
and mistakes so
beautiful that just
for a second, time
ran backwards.
You were part of me,

part of this,
whatever this
turns out to be.
And I'll never
forget that time
we did that thing
that only we
where there
to see,
so thank you.

Joe

Joseph stands. An affront to his life,
mimics actions in order to blend in.
He throws himself through crazy,
says things that are untrue and unkind.

Making sizeable stories seam small,
whilst trying to impress tourists
in smoking bars. The ramshackle
poet...distended from the norms.

His palpable depression interrupting
the aggression. As I tell him off
on the way home at 3am,
so baffled by regularity.

For the cleaning lady will attend
just after 8am and that bitch
is going to be loud,
annoying in every single way.

You see Joe is a fool,
tells stories for impact,
that man you've already seen
that closely resembles me.

Bought Mr. Chinaski
a drink

IT nearly killed me.
The ALL of IT,
the everything-at-once of IT.
Nearly drove me away from rational,
towards excused morning
after night before.
The simplicity of blame
making convenience,
accidentally splendid.

Nearly ran away from
the responsibility of IT,
the maturity of IT.
the never-again of what IT is.
Whittled from pain,
wrapped in given gilded armour,
surrounding the days
with every excuse possible,
as this is the real answer to IT.

The sexuality of IT,
scraping, scratching
depravity of the IT within us all.
Masturbatory gestures,
amid ritualistic excuses
the blanket of normality
entwined our heads to muffle
with the pure narcissistic
nature of IT.

Belly bloated

arm stench

vomiting nature

Of

IT.
This thing we are living.

this upsetting curse

we have been given.

of IT

In It

by IT.

In the middle

I just got annoyed
by the fact that there
is dried red wine
crystallising on the
bottom of our
decanter.

Announce that it
will spoil the next wine.
This, whilst standing
in the middle of my
eleven thousand euro kitchen,
noticing that my BMW
needs to be cleaned and
shouldn't be stood
in direct sunlight.

Then opening another
26 euro bottle of wine,
as my wife returns
from the tennis club

and I realise
just how
middle classed
I really have become.
Retreating to the study
with a glass of
non decanted red,
to pen this.
With not one
single problem
in the world
or excuse
to consider myself
anything but
lucky and privileged
to be positioned
so perfectly
to complain.

Un-wasted

She sits watching a kids TV show
about a talking 'secret agent' mouse.
I sit, attempting to ignore the fact
that we are both wasting our time.

Transfixed, we both know that this
is no good for either of us.
This poem, this episode, are no more
than exhaustion, personified.

Her show takes a turn toward the
surreal, she clutches my arm, as I realise
in my head, I'm writing about a talking
'secret agent' mouse from TV. In some
kids show, as she hides behind a pillow
and I forget about stanza length,
for one sweat second.

I, Break

Three gardeners sit
having a break
on a chipped park bench.

Each, nose deep,
in a smart phone
checking randomness.

In times past
when the city made sense
there would have been banter.

Gentle ribbing and arguing.
Jokey statements
and fat jokes.

Talk of the match on Sunday
one of them not knowing
the pretty pointless scores

They now sitting solitary, having

three separate relationships
with three separate iphones.

Confessing no secrets,
about nothing they've
never even seen.

Waiting for Michael

Waiting for Michael
I wonder
what to say,
what will we talk about?

...Waiting for Michael
I start to question
what's been done,
in time spent.

The nothingness of it all,
the pointlessness of it,
when it's simply done,
the finality.

Even this poem
is something of nothing.
Just waiting for Michael
                    ...whilst thinking.

The Answer...

"God works in mysterious ways"
is the equivalent of a child
putting their fingers in their ears
and stamping their undersized feet
until they get their will.

Explaining nothing,
to no one...childishly.

Arm squeeze

A women came up to me
after a show, a while back,
and said

"You're too big to be a poet,
you look like a bouncer not a thinker"

Unsure how to respond,
I just nodded
and chuckled into my drink.

An Original Bum

As the panic sets in
and the voices start to scream,
I begin my therapy.

Instead of sitting for hours
watching the mindless,
be exactly that.

Instead of finding validation
in the absurdities,
being so beautifully facile.

I attempt originality,
attempt greatness,
even if this is harder to achieve.

Our world is filled with fake news,
eye brow plucked,
rear plumped, non entities.

Holding no control over their
environment, lives becoming no more
than blood money for billionaires.

Kids looking up to the talentless,
persecuting eccentrics because they
broke down or crashed a car.

Adolescence distilled to a pink pills to be
swallowed down with self taken photos
of some girls doctored bum cheeks.

We're worth more than admiring
someone, whose fame comes from
talking to national news about girth.

After sexual indiscretions with a
sports stars or presidents, who has
no recollection of events.

Humanities gift is choice. So let us
choose to hold heroes true, discarding
the chaff like used cigarette butts.

Whilst grasping the slimmest possibility,
that we can do much better than
silicone implants and lies.

Ordinary Kids

Back whilst teaching, I managed
a multi-national English class
filled with mainly Germans
and Swiss kids plus two Asians.

Decided to play the game involving
writing a celebrity's name
on a tiny piece of paper, then
sticking it to another's forehead.
Answering yes or no questions,
in order to resolve.

The class had two, young Chinese
children, who had spent free time
being generally harassed by Euro trash,
whilst beating proud German boys
at table tennis.

I handed out papers
as the specks began to write,
lick and stick. Game starts, room thrusts

into bee buzz stutter and titters.
After ten minutes most of the kids
are finished, guessing film stars
or Pop musicians who can't really sing,
arrogant footballers or
famous politicians.

The only two left are
the two Chinese kids
and the children whom they have
paper stuck. One German child, in
frustration screams;

"Who the fuck is Chen Jingrun?"

(of course in German) His euro friend
does the same, saying

"I've never heard of Yang Liwei" their
annoyance clearly heard.

I walk over to the table
leaning on tired hands, bow head
to deflect situation.

"A great mathematician" says the boy
in perfect English. Sister continues

"and he's an astronaut, first Chinese
man in space"

I look at the two German boys,
annoyed by the Game. Pulling
'Post its' from their heads,
balling and tempestuously throwing
their ignorance to the ground.

Turning my attention back to
the Chinese children, one with 'Justin
Bieber' written on his forehead, "Katy
Perry" scrawled on his sister.

I hang my head to question
definitions of celebrity,
in more systemized cultures.

Who seem to have a better grasp
on what constitutes achievement.

Dance with me

I step inside my madness.
Wear it like gloves.
Each finger stained.
Tick walking father's mimic.

These interruptions of
reality attempt to bridge
restless states of mind,
proscribed sleep adjusted.

This need to move on,
twitching in cold shower
on nights before
this intervention.

Worried loved ones
agree that I've gone
too far, as I roll one up and
retire to an anti room.

Rearranging my pubic hair,
as this seams
the craziest thing
I could do right now.

Your perception is off.
View skewed.
For sanity is mine and
mine alone to dance with.

Gloves now fingerless,
recreating hooves on my desk.
I rest confidently, amongst
these remnants of sanity.

Repeat

Repeat, click, turn page, repeat.

My girl will be different.
A better person.
Although the repeat nature
of the world means
that maybe I should have
thought this through
more thoroughly,
before writing.

Repeat, turn page, click, repeat.

I just go on.
You continue to read,
the same thing
over and over and over,
yet you continue to consume
and I still say no more about
my daughter, just say
the same thing over and over.

Click, repeat, turn page, repeat.

Thus proving that maybe
she won't be different,
maybe nothing really is.
She won't be a better person.
She'll just click, turn page, repeat,
as you are doing right now

as I click, turn page, repeat,

and eventually end.

Beautiful relationship

I spent 47 minutes this morning,
pulling Vaseline infect pubic
root hairs, out of the base
of my penis, after a
five hour drug fuelled
masturbation marathon.

That's the reality of my morning.
Nothing more or less than
exactly that. That's how long
it took to get all of them out.
And there's you thinking this
was going to be a love poem.

Still Done

I'm going to nowhere,
right in the middle of nothing,
to sit and watch no one
do anything at all.

Whilst there, I will talk to nobody,
about nonsense importance's
under no moonlight,
seeing zero stars over head.

Say nothing to an old friend,
who didn't pop by. Not improve
my understanding of the world
nor see impossibilities differently.

Only understand as much
as I presently do.
Amongst no interest in
improving myself at all.

Whilst staying completely still
not listening to the song
of the tiny bird who's
not really there.

Am not going to look
into your eyes
and most defiantly won't tell you
that I love you more.

So why don't you bother
someone else with your questions
and leave me peaceful
in this place I don't really know.

STILL AND QUIET!!!

If you're constantly trying
to improve yourself based on what
other people conceive to be right or
correct. Then how will you ever
understand what is right?

If you never have a quiet moment,
how can you ever
be still enough to comprehend
what you've just done. And why that's
only important to you.

Belly

With these ugly, liver spotted hands,
I now write this directly to you,
as age comes and the possibility of
playing for professional sports vanishes.
As feet grow harder
and browner by the day.
As sounds excrete from every pore
with rise and fall,
hangovers now lasting
best part of a week.
As old friends begin to die,
as we all walk towards prostate exams
and breast smears.
As hair goes grey or falls out.
As previous generations once
nonsense becomes clear.
As we start to wonder about what
will eventually come to us.
As we see the illusion of existence
is so perfectly complete.

As we walk times constructed nature
and true nature's
reconstruction of time.
As we finally understand why our
parents smack our virginal pink asses.
As I sit here and write this with these
tired liver spotted hands,
at forty three years old,
with another 30 to go.

I really wonder if I've
got the stomach for it.

Mean Daddy

After a show I did some time ago,
a young, attractive, women approached.
Book in hand, smile locked.

"I just love your work...I'm such a
massive fan of poetry" she says. "I have
some questions"

"Can I ask you a couple of
questions first?" I ask readying my
pounce, as she nods.

"Who's your favourite poet?"

"Anne Sexton...or maybe
Elizabeth Bishop" she answers, nodding
again.

"So who's your favourite living poet?"
my question receiving a blank stare. This
now unanswered question grates,

fisting want for an answer, that she
can't provide.

"If you're so into poetry who'd
know the name of at least one great
poet working in your lifetime?"

My rooted need to not have this
conversation again, added to thirst
for a cold beer, complete my narcissism.

As she walks away, abashed by my
bullying. Understanding that I'm not a
nice guy...especially when thirsty.

The fact that I'm right
seems to be lost in translations
of which unwritten dreams are made.

She looks back once more, as boyfriend
wraps round her coat and I cheerily
smile, inside my self importance.

Waiting in a bar, to meet an actress

I wonder what this night could bring.
Will reality be altered,
the very fabric of consciousness,
satin scuffed. Meaning found
as drink follow drinks
chat to banter to real connection.
Strobe-lit revelatory conclusions
tossed up and agreed by both.
Follow cocktail, follow shot, follow
laughter...revelations, twinkle, slur.
Walking in imagined parks,
holding minds evolved...as we
tumble through this tryst, so
radiant that we can only
conceive one another fully.
This place found before our feet
now trodden...warn down to
the seed, swallowed and grown.
Aligning the cosmos, conducting

radiance to sing in rapturous
misunderstanding as our minds,
now molten, erupted into
impassioned cliché.

Or,

will I just get drunk and make
a half asses lurch for her breasts?
Tripping over my imagination,
as I stumble back to the gutter.

For God's Sake

If my atheist realisation is wrong,
over decades
of false flag media,
caused by expansive,
mind altering drugs,
experience, science
and commonly known fact.

If God's word
is ultimate truth.
The singular truth
and did create the heavens
and gutters and cancer
and genders and love
and wishes...sorrowful prayers.

If the story be only
the ultimate truth and
definitive word of god, then
there would be only one
biblically magnificent sound.

Not versions of
or may have happened.

If the almighty had but
one word and it was right.
The true voice of god
would be clear.

It's the multiples,
that lead to confusion

and ultimately untruth.

Credentials

Rob...ert Grant.
White,
heterosexual,
male.

I don't care
where you're from,
what colour you are
or who you like loving.

Only care if you
consider other people's
preferences enough,
to not become the problem.

I crave round tits and ass,
in all shapes, sizes,
backgrounds
and colours.

Don't care what you are
or genitals you lick.
It's no business of mine
or anyone's.

That's it for explaining,
now on with something
please anything
more interesting than this.

Puerto Winks

When I first met my wife
twelve years ago now,
I was puzzled why she didn't
know anything about poetry.
Had never read poetry
or preference had.

5 years into our (now)
longer marriage and child,
she comes up to me
at a show that I'm
performing in, nudges me
and whispers...

..."Christ that guy sounds like Whitman"

The sentence itself and
the slightly negative way
she said it, plus the fact that
she finishes with

"He's got the words...

        ...give him five years"

means, that

        she's actually been listening.

Which is beautiful
and makes me want her
more than any man has
ever lusted after their wife.

The price of a beer

Whilst appearing
in a down town theatre
one hot Berlin evening,
forty degree
summer sizzler.

I'm stood at the bar with a
very good American poet
Ben Porter Lewis,
from Ithaca.

A slightly aggregated
weasel of a man
moves around the bar,
fidgeting for attention, lips pursed.

"I know all these guys" he mutters.

"Bob Grant...Ben Lewis.

Hang with all these cats,
been around the scene years now...I run
with all the Beats, the stories man, the
stories."

"Really?" I reply, Ben shuffling over
asking.

"Heard Ben's a dick" his quiet question
unanswered.

"Fancy a beer" I continue, he agrees
and takes one from me, cheers then
sighs aloud.

"He is a bit of a prick, but only if you
don't really know his method."

His response,
draining Ben's sense of humour.
As the bells rings,
for commencement of poetry show.

His face draining, as I'm
stood on stage following
big Ben Lewis
at this wild little reading.

Forever nourished, tingle fed.
Sense of humour
so perfectly formed
in embarrassment.

His uncomfortable squirming,
in those polyester trousers
was really well worth,
the price of that beer.

Scene 17. - Downtown Bar - Night

A beautiful mid-twenties woman (Sarah) kneels in the middle of a pool table. Back arched, ass high, head down, as she lines up her next shot. Her large early forties married friend (Bobby) sits on a side table drinking his 9th beer, after shots, cocktails and other assorted drugs.

Sarah
(Wiggling her perfect ass in the air. Whilst maintaining eye contact with Bobby)

"I feel like going crazy tonight"

Bobby
"I think I should go home"

(Bobby leaves stage right, looking at Sarah's perfect posture the entire way out, bumping into the door frame as he does so, knowing he feels exactly the drunken same)

Hot Dog

One crazy, humid,
midsummer afternoon,
I find myself queuing in a bakery
for a soda and pretzel.
There is only one server
behind the counter
and I'm waiting behind
five assorted types.

The woman in front of me is a
beautiful Greek American girl.
Don't ask how I know she's from
the states, she just oozes New Yorker.
Her strong shoulders, poised stance,
backed up with confident mannerisms
and fashion sense make
my mind straight up.

When her turn comes it's clear to all
that she can't speak a native lick,
stuttering out words as she stumbles

to order a sausage roll and coffee.
Her muscular shoulders contract as a
single bead of sweat rolls between her
perfect shoulder blades, arresting my
attention for a second.

"Eine wurst bitte" I whisper, turning
instantly to romantic hero, that will
guide her through this funny incident
when we met, leading to multiple
orgasms that evening as she
repeats my broken German
to the server, not turning her head
in acknowledgment of my groove.

Starts gesturing and pointing her way
through the rest of the process as
I guide her from behind.
The server asking if she wants
anything else, so I whisper the question
to her neck in German, more sweat
particles forming with the answer.

I say...she repeats, this goes on
as dance. Until, her friend comes in
to lightly tap her shoulder,
using sign language to communicate
with her now obviously deaf friend and
I'm left a misreading fool.

Dancing within his own fantasy...on this
stinking hot Berlin day, in June.

The illusion of it all!

Deep down,
where the dreams don't go
our perception of the world
is proscribed to us
for processing.

Stage one being
the understanding that we
really don't know, nor have
a clarified answer
for anything.

Everything has been
constructed, by us, so as
to explain the unexplainable.
Get a grip on
the real.

Example being, the sun.
We know what it is
what it really is, but

even this is
a mere guess.

For every description
of every-thing existing in
this world we see around us
isn't what we think
it isn't.

The big picture
you are taught to see
may be no larger than a
cancerous wart in the armpit
of some giant.

The time we spend
living our futile existence
is no time at all, for time
is a construct, placed upon us
by astronomy.

This is just phase one.
The fact that I'm describing
this to you is as ridiculous

as any other part of
what's been written.

Effort to help fully
understand anything
is truly futile...a practice of
idiots attempting to
show wisdom or
real truth.

When there's not much
that really needs explaining
in the first place
even words have
their limitations.

For your understanding
of what I have just written
is instantly biased by
your belief of what you
have been told.

Some will read
and scream nonsense,

this guy is clearly a fool.
While others will nod &
hale me some mystic.

When it really,
comes down to the marrow,
these words, these constructions
of symbols, are no time lethargic
'n' don't since make.

So, SMILE
you wasted life amongst
unexplained reason, whilst
riding through nothing
towards no time
at all.

Hung Out

He walks into a bar he knows,
in a time he's experienced.
Presents the cliché
of a drunken poet.
Familiar faces
making him a story teller.
A determined mute,
excused from conversation
due to questions of honesty,
amongst lies about fidelity.
Drunken state precluding
chances chance of
sexual indiscretions,
left silent by the
truth of it all.
Surrounded by strangers
reciting poetry from
a part of his past.
This comfortable anonymity,
the delusion of reason.

For even he doesn't know
why he does it anymore.
The tension created simply
turns heads, adding punctuation
to the emended.
Every drink ordered
brings familiarity to the fact
that he's seen this all before
last week. Confirming the cliché,
the one drunk regular,
that constantly bores tourists
with lofty lies.

Bath time fun

I hear a giggle from the bathroom.

"Papa come here"

says the little naked one, gathering
bubbles round her feet.

"I made you some new hair daddy"

she adds placing bubbles
on my bald spot.

"Papa come closer...come here"

I crouch down prepared for
something cute and innocent.

She then farts and starts hysterically
laughing, which makes her fart again.
This pattern repeating for around 2
minutes or so.

Concluding quickly
with a staunch look and

"Papa...I need a poo poo".

Whilst scrabbling from bath, worried
look on her face, it strikes me as funny
the things that swell pride.

To see her personality forming,
is a beautiful simplicity
only explained by bath farts and bubbles
on Daddy's bald spot.

TV Talent?

I just sat and watched
the new late night TV talent,
eating a bull's penis,
then vomiting into a bucket.

Hoping fully this
is a long term
social experiment.
With order to finding
how stupid and invalid
our societal heroes
have become.

Either that or it's a sign
that this medium
of useless and
meaningless content,
could have fully used itself up.

At That Bar

Late one night,
after another boring meeting
with yet another ego driven,
maniac actress.
I find myself
trudging towards Tomsky,
a bar on Wins Str...Berlin.
I enter and take my usual
position to drink.
Small beer, whiskey no ice
and a glass of tap water.

The bar is filled with
the usual suspects.
My two favourite bar tenders
are doing their best
to judge how crazy
the evening may get
and at what time
(tomorrow morning)
they will be shutting down.

After five minutes or so
of eye fucking
one of the other patrons,
a well kept mid-twenties
man, with a crooked eye
plonks down beside me.

"Wanna see some magic" he asks,
fingering a deck of cards.

"Love to" I reply, excited with prospects.

He then spends
the next hour
drinking and showing
me and some other guy
at the bar, stunning
tricks perfected over
years of practice.
On completion, taking a
seat as he begins
drinking with me.

We talk about everything drunk
people discuss.
He tells me he's
bisexual and has slept
with the bar tender
and how his girlfriend
doesn't know about that.
After more drinking,
shots and drinking,
he puts his beer glass
down on the bar, both
his hand then ending up
on my forearm as he
looks into my eyes
and says

"You know you're...

                              ...very

good looking"

to which, I smile,
the bar tender sniffs
the other laughs
as we all realise

he's hammered drunk
and there is one trick
that crooked eyed magician
wouldn't pull off
this evening...

...at that same bar

...a different night

I again discovered myself
drinking, but this time
I sit, a very drunk
version of the person
formally me.
Start my drunken slobber
on the guy sat next to me
as all my other friends have
already gone home.

"So what do you do?" I ask,
simply because
I love to talk about
poetry, when pissed

and this question
facilitates that
conversation.

"I work in music" he answers,
his small
grey baseball cap
perched perfectly
atop his tinfoil crown.

"Ok" I reply, as I order
my small beer, whiskey
and water, returning to
his conversation, he asks...

"Have you heard that
Cowboy song in the charts?
We were just talking about it"

he looks on for my answer
that comes...

"It fucking haunts my dreams"
I honestly reply,

follow silence and
wry smile, from the
redheaded tender.

'Yes, you guessed it'

I think to myself
in realisation
that he's the guy,
with the perfect
grey baseball cap
that sings that
abomination to music
and now sits
corrupting my atmosphere.

Symmetry

I don't know what it is anymore,
this thing know as love.
I'm scared, so worried
that it turns out to just be a word.
Neither meaning or real understanding,
simply a word.

Vowels and consonants
constructed around a vacuous
sentiment of wishes.
Dreams weaved so neatly as
never to set free real sentiment.
Just a sound,
one last cry of something exciting.

And then she touched me,
everything fell still.
This tryst engorged with possibilities,
made fact by a stolen moment.
Surrounded by drunk strangers
on a night made resolute

by her touch.
Orgasmic throws of symmetry
as we tumble through this testament,
not just a word.
We held our hand entangled
touched each other softly
and quietly screamed...

...This is love

True...or?

Everything I say is a lie
or has elements of untruth.
For you to say otherwise
would mean that
you're lying to yourself,
about me.

Extract from the previous book

Naked

in the

Coffee House

Temporal tin pot

...and so it begins again.
Thoughts corroding reasons,
reasons sculptured into distortions
Rorschach impressions of life.

The past has been drawn to this point
now consuming the present
with future possibilities
fragmenting any want
to continue in a form of now.

For what is, Now?
Is now the experience you are having
in this present tense

but,
by thinking about it in this way
are we not
changing the present
making a new construction of now.

So is it true to say that I am temporal?
Temporally controlled by
knowledge of my past.
Therefore, time is moving
in both directions
and is no more than a
conduit of experience.

If I choose to get run over by a car,
drink a beer, smoke a cigarette.

The past effects the present
in the same way as the present
effects the future
for time is merely an illusion,
existence is all there ever has
or ever will be
striding toward a memory of
even writing this.

Do I stop here?
                    ...or here?

Or continue writing
until the ink runs clear
paper becomes extinct.

Do I stop mid sentence...

                    ...to simply confuse.

If time be truly temporal
and there is <u>only</u> this moment
existing in the mind.

Then maybe this poem
should go on forever
and we should all fuck,
extremely slowly.

Creating the Cover

by artist

Georgia Krapf

Being given only the reference of his title "Beat the Grass….to startle the snake" the design process began. Through many iterations, long nights, crazy rants, conversations about life, and truly reading his words lead us to find his cover.

 My process began with a light fixture that has a strong spotlight quality, strong, determined, it knows what is it. I aimed the spotlight at a dress form and sketched a silhouette of a woman/every woman/everyone. I wish it to represent a person/people/humanity. In its woman form, I chose to portray it in line work and detail lines to try and capture the way I feel society drives us. Longs legs, round ass, slim waist, perfect shape breast, straight back, jewellery around the neck, and blank above.

This form is the only view of the true origin of material represents true nature, naivety, beautifulness, and complexities of all the working parts. All of the media background represents the minutia of daily life and the overwhelming screen of capitalism.

It is the way we are told to be, what is supposedly the best for us, who to love, what to eat, and what is the most beautiful.

There is so much bombardment and intensity here. People are spoon fed this way, every day, and all the days. Can one wake up from this? In reading through the book, the poem "Waiting for Morning" is one of many that really resonated with me and this media background. I loved the last stage of this piece because it was to capture the play of light and come back to the spotlight.

I choose to invert the dark shadow to white for many reasons. I see the shadow/whitewash as contextually enlightened consciousness and awareness. It's not the bandwagon and what everyone else seems prescribed to. The white space is a peace, a contentedness that I have always strived for and will continue to fight for.

On the books cover it manifests itself as an Ouroboros painted figure that represents this infinity or wholeness. The shape also references ensō, which is when the mind is free to let the body create.

This childish scene, we all play out,
these hurtful words we say.
Never knowing what they fully mean
or which order they should be said.
In the blink of one pink eye you're done,
left, holding a bag full of dirt...

...Now run those damaged red green lights,
turn air in your lungs to hurt.